Acid Rain Epithalamium

Poems
Becca Downs

Beyond The Veil Press

Acid Rain Epithalamium
© 2026 Becca Downs
Cover Design © Becca Downs

ISBN: 979-8-9943727-3-9

Second Edition, 2026

First Edition, 2024
Beyond The Veil Press

Edited by Tyler Hurula

Interior & Cover Layout by Sage Herrin
Mr Bitey Logo by Josiah Callaway

Created on the lands of the Kumeyaay/Kumiais peoples, in the so-called United States. Visit https://native-land.ca/ to see whose land you are on.

TABLE OF CONTENTS

INTRODUCTION

Might a divorce, like a wedding, require ceremony, witnesses, vows taken? The poems of Acid Rain Epithalamium become songs for the dissolving of an important bond out of which the speaker reemerges forever changed, fragmented into a choir of selves. One self explores pleasure inside her queerness; another one seeks a starker and more sustaining relationship with the divine; another traces the precious and precarious interconnections between the self and other living beings: plant, animal, and mineral. Watch how the poet unravels the wedding dress to thread a vivid fabric using the warp and weft of the poem. With a "word turned hurricane" the reader witnesses a new vow taken with the ancient art.

–Carolina Ebeid, author of You Ask Me to Talk about the Interior

Acid Rain Epithalamium is the place between grieving a withered promise and letting go of an evaporated future. Becca puts their wedding dress in a box and begins to pick through the wreckage to create a new self. They interrogate one of the very real dilemmas of our generation: do we procreate or protect our planet? What do we do with a future we never asked for?

I've read a lot of divorce memoirs, but it wasn't until Acid Rain Epithalamium (queer chaos, gender rebel, relationship anarchy) that I found a story similar to mine. It gives me hope that I might recover from my own divorce and find sunlight again. Becca's work employs stunning nature imagery–storm clouds, cornfields, summer rain– rooted in a strong sense of place. Plus, an arsenal of clever forms to keep us engaged. Acid Rain Epithalamium is something you must experience. These poems are both baptism and rebirth.

–Sage Herrin, poet & EIC of Beyond The Veil Press

To everyone who sent a wedding gift,
please consider this the Thank You card
I couldn't bring myself to write before.

Acid Rain
Epithalamium

HER INTO HIMSELF

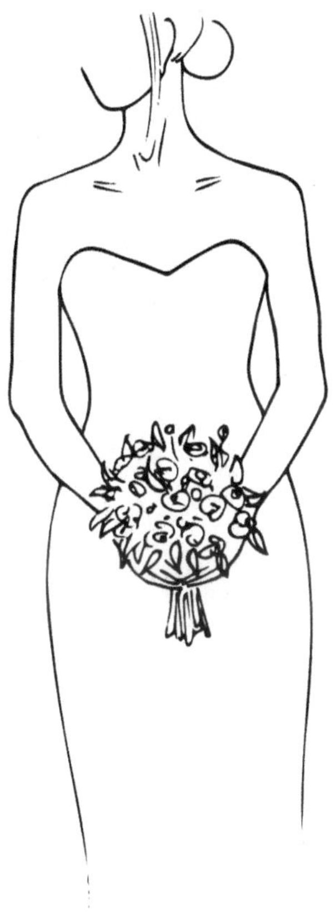

Becca Downs

Her into Himself

Must a river
stop being
a river
the moment she
meets the sea?
Could she
continue
her path
through ocean's
lapping waves,
or does she
lose integrity
once he spits
his salty
sea breath
on her face?
The river
does not slow—
she rushes
forward, albatross
caught in a gale,
then leaps
into his jaws
as he roars,
chews, digests
her into himself.

The Last Wedding Gift
an anti-epithalamium

I've been measuring nights, they are never the same
    long, sleepless, thick whiff of nightmareseven wide eyed
    long, bouts of terror
    short, sleepless
    full of sleep without rest.

I've been measuring days, too
How long it takes til I think of you
    scent on street corners
    dust under my bed
    sharp cabinet edges
    word turned hurricane

Night or day, long or short
I wrestle with you, our sheets
    porcelain bedding
    wedding gift
    ours now mine

What is a sheet but a ghost
    muffling midnight
    a surrendering
    fresh page
    for full revision

But ours now mine shrieks
    the kind of phantom
    to push me down
    a flight of creaking stairs

I know, I counted each step.

Together we torched everything
    we once touched, but the sheets
    on my bed remain uncharred
    forgotten lace lingerie
    grown cold and too much

The nights would measure the same I believe
if I could singe the damn sheets
that last shaded snowpile in spring

in a box / in the closet

<table>
<tr><td>

old
letters he
addressed
and sent too late
came
too late,
my wedding dress
decaying in a box

</td><td>

love
found other
half-naked
(to kiss)
(in secret)
too soon,
my broken heart
hidden in the closet

</td></tr>
</table>

di-vorce

/də-vôrs/
late Middle English
from Latin divortium
(see divert)

1. noun: the legal dissolution of a marriage by a court or other competent body
   as in, "her husband had an affair then asked for a divorce"
   as in, "the Catholic church condemns divorce"
   as in, "ultimately, she filed for divorce because he was too cowardly to do it himself"

2. noun: a separation between things which were or ought to be connected
   as in, "she contemplated a divorce with the Church"
   as in, "she wondered if it is even a divorce if two things ought never to have been connected in the first place"

3. verb: legally dissolve one's marriage with (someone)
   as in, "they divorced after three months of marriage"
   as in, "when they divorced, she paid a lot of money for his selfishness, but not as much as he did"

4. verb: separate or dissociate (something) from something else
   as in, "she divorced herself from the belief that God would gatekeep eternal life just because a human man was scared of the life he had on earth"
   as in, "she divorced herself from every belief she ever had so she could start anew"

5. adjective: of or relating to divorce
   as in, "she has a business card in her wallet for a great divorce lawyer"
   as in, "she looks glamorous in her divorce jacket that she bought with divorce money"
   as in, "divorce she is divorce going to the divorce store to pick up divorce groceries to make a divorce dinner alone in her divorce apartment before drinking a glass of divorce wine and crawling into her divorce bed and turning off her divorce light so she can dream divorce dreams or stare at her divorce ceiling until her divorce alarm relieves her"

as in: The divorce between the woman and (someone/something) caused the woman to divorce herself from (things) and now she writes divorce poems in her divorced head while she divorce sleeps in her divorce sheets and counts like sheep every(thing) else she wants a divorce from.

Child Bride
Ring of Sonnets

You're claiming inheritance, after all,
in a dove-like dress you'll wear like water,
face warm as inside of prayer-folded hands,
toes scrunching in time with passion wailing
from your penny-sized mouth for newborn fear
for this wash of tepid, blessed water
falling above you, washing your forehead.
Hear the monotony from the priest
when he says: I baptize you in the name
of the Father, and of the Son, and of
the Holy Spirit. Just like that, Child
Bride, you were most graciously rid of your
hideous Original Sin. Like that,
you were reborn, ready to live. Amen.

Upon Examining My Collection of Empty Bird Cages

My childhood plays like a vignette
of family videos recorded in strange
moments, like the choice to record
an afterthought: I bask in the sunlit
memory of the unfiltered first grader
who stood up during reading time
to correct a boy's mispronunciation;
the second grader who decided to be
the sole cellist in the school, lugging
a coffin-like case on the crowded
bus twice a week; the third grader
who danced while she performed
her saxophone solo, who requested
of her teacher a restraining order
from the squirrely boy who wouldn't.
stop. touching. her.
and the fourth grader who took
matters into her own hands
kicked a handsy boy in his shins
and watched him cry in the hallway.

Then the memories blend
finger paint to nail polish
without distinguishing when.

I recall giggles, blushing
cheeks, notes, awkward
phone calls after dinner,
tears, and the feeling like
your insides are pushed
off a cliff. I try to piece
the memories in place
like I'm solving a puzzle
to determine when I decided
to lure the men I loved
into cages, and lock
myself in with them.

Becca Downs

At the Feet of Desire
two golden shovels after Joy Harjo

It is never too late for the i
in married to yield, lay
flat like a worm at
my feet, exit entirely from the
word, so the other letters sans feet
can rest to express the aftermath of
an incomplete depletion of desire,
a scratch in the record for
which we'll mark our sullied years.

***

There is no I
in feet, though I had
used mine frequently, followed
an archaic map to desire,
the i which lead me to
a union in a quiet canyon, the
unmarked gap at the map's end.

Lost Goodbye

the morning I left the clouds
hovered so thick, overlapped
like trees in the backcountry,
I couldn't see the mountains

between you and me I could
only catch vague city shapes
in the rearview mirror, only
small stretch of cement ahead

it's the mountainsI'll miss,
I held, but they didn't send me
off, and of all the lost goodbyes
that one is nearly the worst

Caged-Tiger the Tide Pools

I swim your skin
like so many tide pools
        stitched between rocks,
                move up your arms, meld us
                        no matter how far apart our eyes rest
                                from each other's hearts, raking dark ceilings—
                                black canvas skies upon which we imprint stars,
                                animate a show of shooting then vanishing.
                        Awe lurches from my chest—
                        a caged tiger eager to pounce
                        at the faintest breath.

I Michelangelo my ceiling.
I caged-tiger the tide pools.

I finish pawing
empty sheets—
        blank letters stitched,
                one long, pining thought
                        aggressively unwritten.

Big Shoes

Thousands of people claw each other boarding airplanes to escape the new regime. Some don't make it. The airplane takes off but the passengers don't know if they will be welcome when the airplane lands. We've seen this scenario since long before someone successfully flew and landed an airplane (that was 1903). Now Airplanes have big feet. That is, airplanes have the largest carbon footprint. They're the least environmentally-conscious form of travel for vacationers. Want to escape the city? Walk to the country. Talk to the farmers. If you ask them, things aren't going so hot. It's too hot. Last summer the Bay Area saw orange skies all day. Wildfires destroyed homes and farms and lungs. Out east the sunsets were breathtaking, but in Colorado you could hardly draw breath or see the sun. Someone's son was shot there and we read about it in the news. Saw the tweets, the hashtags. His murderers wear badges and carry guns in public, ask us what we were wearing when we were attacked, unleash tear gas on peaceful protesters. That summer we had time to be tear gassed in the streets because a microscopic murderer spread death on tables, on hands, through our coughs and our hugs. The murderer wore our grandma's gray curls, our uncle's bow tie, our children's tear-filled eyes, our lover's lips. The murderer punished the poor, the lonely, the essential. No one wants to work anymore. Communism is trending, along with red lipstick, nose rings, picket lines, and knitted mittens. Napping is an act of resistance. The enemy is capitalism. The enemy is your neighbor. The enemy is a stranger having a bad day online. The enemy broke into your home in the middle of the night to stick your fingers in water. The enemy did the same to a stranger but took his child, too. That child lives in a cage with other children. That child can't board an airplane, but maybe one day, she thinks, she'll grow some wings and become an airplane herself. Those are big shoes to fill. When the world burns completely she'll fly a little higher to glimpse the sun above the smoke.

Planting Seeds

in the day I clutch
my stomach, imagine it

empty

in the night I clutch
my stomach, imagine it

full

Made Mountains of Marriage

he married   me

for as short as he could,

making us both confused

questioning the purpose-

how three months home

smoke out before us, me

a cracked sidewalk puddle,

both   broken & knowing

he   loved   her

then like a breeze he left

her place, left her lost in

full mountains we climbed

made of our   marriage

well   behind   him now,

and her a foothill trampled

him traveling on unscathed

Child Bride, Age 7
Ring of Sonnets

You were reborn, ready to live. Amen.
In a little white gown, white lace veil
gazing up at a man in a black suit,
white rectangle under Adam's Apple.
But he is not a man, we are told, he
is our Father, a representation
of THE Father, a mouthpiece, holy as
matrimony, baptism, as today's
First Communion. Child who looks
like a bride, enjoy the photos, the cake,
the gifts: the pearl rosary from Grandma,
porcelain angel figurine, the book
of saints, white beaded purse. Enjoy it all–
marriage is long, so many don't make it.

12 trash bags

that's how many we filled
before selling our house

by "12" I mean
it could be any number

by "filled" I mean
stuffed like taxidermied game

by "selling" I mean
desperate, for less than listing

by "our" I mean
my ex husband's and mine

by "we" I mean
his mother and me

by "trash bags" I mean
body bags sounded dramatic

by "that's" I mean
I am trying to be real with you

by "many" I mean
few

by "house" I mean
event horizon

by "before" I mean
the burning out of we/our

by "how" I mean
what follows me everywhere

Becca Downs

Bring Me Your Dead Already

She sends me flowers
dead, pressed in pages
of letters she writes and
I love her for the gesture.

Not the flowers or letters
as much as the feeling of being
so known. Fresh cut flowers
fuel my dopamine

crashes—how often
have I plucked sweet
lilacs on spring days
when I'm in love or hope

to be, then spent hours
lamenting the broken stems
left behind—and she knows
this, not every flower

I've slaughtered, but
that their vase-life
is short and I struggle
accepting it. Forget-

me-nots dried and placed
like delicate confetti in an envelope
won't decay before my blind eye.
Bring me your dead already

long dead so I know what
to do with it.
She's come to know I hold
onto things far past their

expiration—letters and flowers,
my love and my regret, yes
my hate, and the seasons
of "you" littering my confessions

like fallen petals strewn
beside those spilled from envelopes
she sealed with her tongue
while she thought of me

—all of which feels like
the same singular thing clenched
tight in my letter-writing hand
begging me to let go

Acid Runoff

We sleep in
a bed of roses
fed runoff

acid from power
plants and human
tears, we sweat
and spit it

we are breathing
poison machines
waiting, preying

everything wet
about us is tainted
won't grow how
it used to

we are watching
earth sleep on
a bed of bent
backwards fluorescent

flowers, praying
she will wake
the way sun breaks
a dragging night

how we release
a long-held breath
or belief

when a lover comes
home or when
they leave for good.

Real, and Here

I fall frequently drunk
on moonlight
so I won't thirst
for the sun

the sun a drug
with withdrawals
like earthquakes
and monsoon rain

the moon in daylight
taunts,
pulls rope taut,
says tug a side

I look to clouds
for help
but they can't
hear me, or won't

waste the wind
on prayers
paid with a fist-
ful of rhinestones

& I can't blame anyone
for wanting
the real thing, diamonds
in a satin sky

a river frigid
from winter melt,
a ghost voice
made real, and here

Becca Downs

Split

No one will buy the wedding dress
that became a corpse since we became
the sound of shredding

Sunday psalms. A gorgeous garment
tainted by the way we split–

an atom
the last piece of cake
half of my shit and half of his.

I see when people look at me
like I'm half
of something beautiful and better

but know this: he spared my body
when he severed
our hallowed bond. Look:

the other side of my bed
is not a funeral. Goldenrods grow
in this chapel. Purple astor births
more of itself.

I didn't split like any thing.
I split like a getaway driver,

my side, tossing laughter
carefree with hometown hands
on streetlamp nights

feeling myself delicious,
new wisdom and new hair,
new names dripping from my lips

a love letter ripped from the binding
of a notebook, my own laugh,
sounds that pop like fireworks.

Two of Us in This Grave
a golden shovel after Lisel Mueller

What could possibly be hiding there
worth pulling back the curtains? Are
loose coins lost worth two
times the ones in your pocket? Of
all the lies we believed, us
lingered longest. It lies here
in this grave at my feet now. Touch
the headstone. It reads: always with me.

Becca Downs

The Shape of Things

Is it so strange to wonder at your own god-
like powers to change the shape of things,
invisible things like Anger and Longing?

to imagine disputes caged in only your mind,
write them down and breathe life into them,
build a city tooth and nail where they may roam,
then dismantle that world's brittle infrastructure?

how newspapers build stories you can see
and toss in a fire to watch disappear—
how like a sponge you hold those stories
saturated heavy with Tragedy and Pride,
how they alight gold in the licking flames
then crumble like a cremating body—
how the ashes settle in the silent dark
until swept up in a sudden gust of wind
or nudged by a gentle breath, a whisper
from a ghost, a voice like someone
you once knew, hushing your name.

BURNING AGE

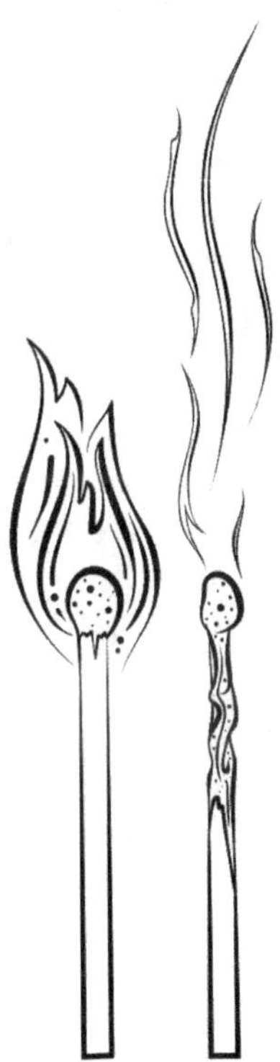

Becca Downs

Burning Age

What is the technical difference
between curling fog and smoke
-show, us, honey, our lonely stone-still eyes
that can only watch as plumes consume trees
outside your parents' air-conditioned living
room, and the forgotten Sunday scents of
a sunrise while we're stone-scared at the pyre
waiting for a sign, smoke after a house fire
a gravestone properly crumbled for its years
anything to keep us wondering: what happens

I asked you, my love, doe-eyed
when we were so young, sixteen and sure,
how to unclasp the intricate back
collapse those musty car seats we burden
breathing engines whirring, because to have
someone else on our lips would douse us
of sacred passion for this burning age
marking the transition to a mature phase
or pretending we've found balance
between new flames and unearthed rage

Awakening, Again

This is the room where I sleep,
where I eat bread and butter,
where I cry to God and myself.

This is where I stare at the ceiling
and direct films to replace horror
with romance, comedy with comedy.

This is the window where I watch
squirrels chase other squirrels.
It's new. Before there were no windows.

This is the lamp that started
as a flashlight that started
as a candle that started
as a match that took sleepless weeks to light.

Before then, this room was dark.

Before the window
and the match
I could only see
the thin dim golden
glow under the door.

I kept time with footsteps—
visitors, well-wishers, friends.
I think it was a friend who slipped
the match under the door.
I'd never lit a match before,
But once flame flickered
at my fingertips
I knew I could light a candle.
Once I lit a candle,
I knew I could illuminate
the floorboards before my feet.
From there, my pupils
constricted like pools of water
under summer sun.
This is how my life began again,
how my life always begins
again and again—
with a slim ray of gold light,
an eyelid upon waking.

Becca Downs

Drive Like Your Children Live Here

I wear a No Outlet sign around my neck like a cross.
I am constantly under construction.

I swallow nothing down my throat,
spit out breath that tastes like stale prayer.

What good am I to a dying planet?

To bring a child into the world is to force
at least one death.

I am a child myself, have always been
a child and might always be
so I tell myself a child should not take
care of another child, that Mary was a child
and from her womb bloomed
deadly dogma.

Children like me drive past children
who can't yet drive, who chase
each other like good dreams
in their kingdom of cracked streets,
scream with the birds
and wave to strangers.

I tell myself I know what they mean,
parents who commission
Drive Like Your Children Live Here signs.
Drive like confessing your sins
to a towering man scowling.
Drive like contritions never given
audience. Don't drive like your mother
that time your nose gushed blood
and wouldn't stop. Like your mother
holding you while you heave in panic
from bad dreams that hide in closets
and under your bed. Hide in your mother's
closet and under her bed, haunt her too.
Your mother is a child herself.
Don't drive like your mother
screams in labor with the future of this sighing
planet. I wave back to the children.

I wonder if the secret
is Share the Road with the future,
every blade of grass that has brushed
human flesh. Breezes that shuffle
hair and breath like desert rain.
My jokes and wails and the Hail
Marys I whisper in secret
when I crawl into bed.
Everything we touch or say
or swallow is holy.

I take the pill like eucharist
in the driver's seat of my dusty car,
parked beside debris and abandoned bottles,
dawn glaring gray in the Walmart parking lot.
I weep ripping open the package,
throw back the lone pill, choke
down this act of mercy and love
for a drying planet.

I tell myself this incantation, this prayer,
this wine gulp might wash down
the lump in my throat
      that has hovered
      for years like a pill
      stuck.

The Magician's Secret

in the darkest hour of night

I pull sleep   from my hat

and every   time   find   it

turns out a   dead rabbit

Child Bride, Age 14
Ring of Sonnets

Marriage is long, so many don't make it.
You wear a frilly white dress and gold ring
dutifully on your right ring finger
bearing Virgin Mary in the form of
Miraculous Medal, a gift from your
mother to celebrate the occasion
of your Confirmation, marked by your young
declaration of obedient faith
to the Church, to the Father. O Mary,
Conceived without sin, pray for us that we
may be made worthy of the promises
of Christ. O Mary, remind me to be
a good daughter. To my parents. I mean
to the Church. Obedient to the Church.

Alimony

or Someone Said I Wasn't Angry Enough

I killed a man once

with kindness
he did not deserve.

He's dead now

to me.
I do not regret

the kindness I gave—

it dressed like sunlight
peeking around naked trees,

sounded like the first shooting

star I ever saw.
I can't afford

rent or to forget,

so kindness is my currency
and he's been paying for it

in cash

since the day
he left.

Borders

I understand borders the way
I understanda religion—lines
drawn to teach us what is wrong,
songs to swell hearts with pride,
to hide the complexities of ideals—
       that is to say
concepts aren't purebred horses,
aren't evenly divisible by any number,
can't disappearwhen you close
your eyes and cover your ears—
with every year that passes voices
       lift like heat from pavement, seeking
             to strip lines we thought etched
                    like tattoos on the Body, but actually
               arbitrarily pinned, arrogantly stained
                     on rocks and rivers closer to God
                     than you or I have ever been.

Becca Downs

What Else

I am less
aimless
I am inside
a one-bedroom
I am one
I am girl
in love
with girl
I am sick
everyone is sick
I am fraction
of one piece
on couch
staring out
the window
hair on floor
mopping tears
I am not
girl, not
in love
with boy
still, I am
scrolling
through too much
news,
I am human
wondering who else
is human too
I am tired
of trees burning
like words
in picket lines
I am one
sign, signing
in/out
I am breath
barely, and heart
I am bare,
barren,
brief for fear
everyone will stop
listening
before I reach
the end
the one where
I reveal
what else
I am
I am not
there yet

yolk

my hand holds
a cracked eggshell
crying
into my palm
like a child
feeling her first
brush of bitter
winter wind

my hand knows
to create
something new:
discard
the shell,
and the yolk
is free
to transform

Lullaby

in my sleep strangers grab my wrists and pull //me behind a veil that turns into //a wall when i wake, lure me with starry //skies and promises that smell like a night //we might have shared, or dreamed of once, whisper //secrets and wrap my shivering body //in a thin sheet, because even here i //can't imagine something more for myself //one by one they kiss my cheek, each stranger //then vanish or shift into another //stranger, one who looks like someone i once //shared a bed and dishware with, one who shares //dishware elsewhere in the world with someone //else. i see them beyond the next veil //one i can't reach. i see them hand-in-hand //their shoulders leaning in toward each other //like an A-frame house remains when sleep fades //and the veils turn into walls again //their silhouettes turning two human shapes //to one sings me back to daylight, just like //lullabies we didn't know were about //dead children.

Bride, Age 29
Ring of Sonnets

To the Church? Obedient to which church?
Again white dress, in the Redwoods gleaming
at your lover under towering trees
as tall as God herself, as fragile as
a field of matches in dry season.
A hippie woman recites love poems,
you and your love recite eternal vows.
On your left fourth finger your love places
what once belonged to your grandma's finger,
a pearl and diamond ring, a symbol of
endless devotion. You tether a ring
to him, kiss, swear this feels holier
than any Cathedral. A prayer: you swear
it over and over to make it true.

Becca Downs

Wall Sway Holding

One night that wouldn't end I heard
a loud rumble and the bedroom walls
swayed. No one was there to hold
my hand because I thrust my heart
upon a man who treated marriage
and divorce as bookends to therapy
he was always late to. Someone's child
might have died that day, but I've been
too busy licking my wounds to consider it.
Tongue smoother than baby skin now.

I am grieving a past and mourning
a future, so to live I am clasping hands
with the present. Look, she sends velvet
red petals for my fingers to brush. Gold
leaves laden at my feet. Mountain breezes
chilled from snow-melt. Sun rays spotlighting
my eyelids with each blink.

A thousand miles and three years west
a wildfire hitched a ride with the wind
and bulldozed suburban neighborhoods
unaccustomed to the kind of heat
that turns dining tables into a bed
of broken glass. Shards of windows
where a hot meal should be. Building
ashes settled on sidewalks where children
rode bikes. Now they look out unfamiliar
windows to check for apocalyptic orange
skies, sniff the air for signs of choking
smoke. It wasn't supposed to happen there.
Who knows where a disaster will haunt
someone's children next.

In this moment, someone smokes a joint
and the scent perfumes my hair. He nods
as he passes under the same sun rays.
In this moment, a caterpillar inches the porch
railing. A landline rings in my memory, but
there are no landlines anymore. In this moment,
my phone vibrates—a call from someone
with good or bad news, a voice in any case
that reaches out like a warm hand holding
mine, that would hold it even as walls sway
and houses burn.

Becca Downs

Lunar Healing

i. waning

I'd prefer not to share
what I've done in the dark

nor what I've seen by light
of anything that burns.

The moon may sway a mood
but not the hand that holds

the knife

ii. new moon

I walk in the day as a sensible woman.
Instead of hearing hooting owls

blue jays highlight branches
before me, zip deeper in the trees.

It's late March and daffodils bloom
in unexpected yielding

yellow patches.
I marvel at the winds that spread

seeds accidentally
among tree roots, along easements.

At night my sight is skewed
by everything a sensible woman knows,

but like any sensible woman
I see the world in light and wonder

is this what the new moon spies
without the sun in her eyes?

iii. waxing

We can endure a multitude
of deaths, divorce being one—

a cloaked figure comes to reap a body whole
but leaves clutching bloody parts

of beating hearts that never regenerate
the same in the bodies still breathing

Aubade for a Body

When golden
blades of light
slice our sleep
with morning
please leave
nothing
in your wake
but space
where your scent
mingled with my
sheets,
let me believe
I am nothing
but a ten
digit sequence
you'll never see
again,
like this exact
sunrise, spilling
dust particles
in the shadows,
swirling
with invisible
currents, landing
crouched and
untouched
in the cracks
and corners
of my body
my bed,
this body
bag bedroom.

Love, (a) (Bi)sex(ual) (Wo)man

I am so(rry)-scared
he is my (de)fault.

Every (wo)man before
has fit securely (t)here.

I'm not (k)new
to seeing bare flesh

as a (wel)come
mat.

Grab my (hand)some-
thing, (what)ever

you seek, and drown
(me) in your (he)art.

He(lp) (d)is(card) my
(de)fault,

this is the real me(ss)
we all lie (in).

Becca Downs

No Name Here

a pastiche of Saeed Jones' "Alive at the End of the World"

A gathering of heartbeats is called
a family, a home, or a threat,
depending on where they drum
in relation to red lines, red refracting
rays, or red hills

depending on where their ancestors
once picked fruit and held hands
and prayed, or
who is clutching the neck
of a stethoscope.

One heartbeat is called life,
but two heartbeats in one body
is called a miracle or a murder,
depending on how heavy
clouds hang on the horizon,

what that heartbeat
might inherit: generations
of violence given or violence
taken, of violence of violence
of violence liquid on the tongue.

Heartbeats in harmony
with the deep bass burdening
corkboard streets at night
know no one has ever cared
how quiet a heart can be,

heartbeats know nothing
but yes, no, and almost, baby, almost,
heartbeats howl at the moon
while a uterus strips naked
strip teases for freedom

the humanity granted daylight
in a room full of assault
rifles heartbeats break
the silence of quivering fear, still
heartbeats have no name no name no name here

Cetaphobia

I've never been keen on seeing any whales.
As a child my noodle legs flailed wild,
chin tapped waves, and the gap
where a tooth once lived felt the rush of saline.
I waded past the point where my feet
could touch the smooth, sandy
floor, where my dad stood like a statue,
when he asked me to swim,
 show how I had learned at the neighborhood pool.
But the pool hid nothing
at all times, while the ocean kept
a large galaxy of secrets.

I'm afraid I'll see a whale.
It wasn't my business how the largest creature
known to child spent its time
in the dark depths of an unfathomable universe.

Sometimes in adulthood,
standing tall while waves
of grief and guilt penetrate
the shield my teeth makes
for the back of my throat,
when someone wants to spill
the contents of their heart to me,
share their behavior
when no one was around,
secret self,
I don't know what to say.
What could someone's massive
mischief do once awakened?
Lost hooks sink to the ocean floor,
catching dinner for something else.

Becca Downs

Children

a pastiche of Maggie Smith's "Bride"

How long have I been fed
of the earth? Calling her

mother, if thinking
to call at all.

Choosing perfume to turn
blame for how long I have been

ruining her house, but not
alone. Marred less

by men and women
than silverhaired corporations.

I know the kind of fuel
I am to become:

the kind who will leave
earth the same instant

we all do. We are colic
in the smoke we made veiling

her face. Mother, we cry,
have we wasted your one life?

Modern Love/Climate Disasters

It doesn't usually look like this. Mountains cloaked in cloud cover, no layers of blue arches to texture the sky behind the cityscape. Wildfires rage somewhere west of here, so today we breathe thick—fog, smog, or white flags overhead and as far as we could normally see. Normally, a cartoon-perfect sky. Jagged peaks behind coffee shops and restaurants and rooftops and every other shape that makes a city. A cactus here, generous splashes of sunflower everywhere. But now, gray haze. Ghostly veil obscuring landscape. And I, a visitor, imagining the blue they say sings the sky at all other times. It's not normally like this. Your bedroom, you mean. Clothes coat the floor like heavy snowfall, cover your bed like a tornado you slept through. I'm embarrassed, this is a mess. I didn't expect to bring you here like this. You clear just enough space for us on your bed and we make love anyway. The next morning haze lingers over mountains, mountains of clothes still haze the carpet, mine mingle now with yours, and I want to tell you, I don't normally do this. Sleep with someone I'm not seeing, that is. Shed myself. Mix my mess with someone else's. Linger too long. Smoke sweet lovers out oftheir own homes. Wonder what color the sky might be this afternoon or ten years from now.   Linger too long.

Becca Downs

Peace Offerings

it's early enough
windows still black
I see myself
when I flip the switch
so quiet I can hear
faint buzzing
of kitchen light

heat cranks on,
down the street
a dog barks
to be let inside
I can't hear the door
but it's quiet again
and I imagine her
at the foot of a man

outside the wind presses
its face to my kitchen
window, envious
of steaming coffee
and my gentle aloneness–
I can't see him
but I know his scent,
feel his cheek on mine

I'm reminded of doves
how they're never late,
not really,
and the odor
of olives rotting,
shriveled on a branch
half-forgotten, perhaps
in a box in my closet.

I stand at the window
so long my face
fades with pre-dawn
black, morphs
into a fence,
a small tulip tree
budding like a teen,
a garden plot waiting.

ACID RAIN EPITHALAMIUM

Becca Downs

Acid Rain Epithalamium

this isn't the rain we asked for
it runs like lava down leeward
rocks,   seizes   the cities, it
looks like smoke   sizzles
on pavement like hot grease
but   might it still wed weeds
to soil might corn still marry
earth & sky in late july could
it still caress valleys   soak
hollers   dress mountains
in a technicolor coat of wild-
flowers   temper flames
that torch the mountainsides
could the children still grow
healthy & tall   soft-skinned
& singing to open acrid sky
this isn't the rain we asked for
but it is the rain we've made
love to   dropped to one
knee bound ourselves for life
this could be   a celebration
windborn   praise songs
crawling toward mountaintops
bodies dancing by moonlight
bring your pots to the bonfire
let us boil what drips off eaves-
troughs into our gaping mouths

Woman as Cloud Performer

Before breath
I was girl.
Then I grew
and became: performance

the way clouds
form from water,
become cookiecutter
shapes we can name.

I wailed under bright lights.
That fright
my first lesson
in staging.

Do clouds hear
the names we give them
and shape-
shift to something else?

Now I am girl only
when no one watches,
water droplets dancing
when they do.

Holy at the Crossroads

Forgive me, Father, for I have
caress of curve and edge

my body, the way wind
presses to every part, rushing

river or quiet pond
draws in to cover up, consume-

mate moonlight. If a night together
drowns like that, let it be

my end. Let hands feel shoulder,
breast, waist, hip, thigh like running

water, then like gust of wind
sweep back up. Let hands rest

in slope of lower back.
To breathe in someone

else's heavy shaking
exhales, to soak in sweat

drenched desire, eyes
reading eyes—holy as breaking

bread or anything else earth
or breath could offer.

Praise the unraveling road
for intertwining mine with

another's for any brief hours
we can lay palm to palm, brush

fingertips, whisper magic
spells meant only for our ears.

Child Unbride, Ages 30+
Ring of Sonnets

Swear over and over to make it true.
Now, the Virgin Mary dwells on my left
middle finger, and that's not tongue-in-cheek
but an aesthetic move I made after
I removed my wedding ring the day he
asked for a divorce. My grandmother's ring
is in a box, perhaps in my closet.
I cannot divorce myself from this piece
of her memory I have. I cannot
divorce myself from the masochism
of holding onto things that won't hold me
back, like water cannot divorce herself
from the fall. Unless a drought consumes us,
I'm claiming inheritance, after all.

Becca Downs

All Life
another golden shovel after Joy Harjo

Close your eyes. Consider the praise
that brushes like a ghost past you in the
morning hours while light rain
buries your lover's breath, carries it
instead through the bedroom door, brings
it to settle in an untouched corner more
dust than dark. Consider the rain;
how it plagiarizes the praise
songs another sings to us, rinses the
room clean and leaves you wanting rain
still, because even when it drenches it
rings like a songbird, sometimes brings
your lover's voice along, lifts more
than eyelids, reminds you all life is rain.

Ravishing

It's in their eyes:
they want to close in
like hyenas,
seize what they can
from the lone woman
drinking in this bar:
brace for impact,
wonder this time how
to say I'm more
interested in the woman
with jet black hair
in a knot on her head,
whose manhole eyes lock
with mine each swing
of the kitchen door:
I want to order
more food just to see
sweat dripping down
her neck again.
Door swings:
brace for impact:
the men are hungry.

Becca Downs

A man explained consciousness & ego at me & now I'm thinking about a handmade table 1,300 miles away

do you think
it's feeling right now?

cold wind seeping through window cracks
bearing icy tidings from Superior shores.
memory of touch, a child's hands
sticky with oatmeal and strained
with absorbed fidgets of unfinished meals,
a boy waiting to run free
outside with the weeds & summertime bees.

do you think it
envies? misses?
forgets? do
you think it could
shed, in its way,
tears for every day
it sits untouched?
find comfort in
other fixtures
saturated with their
own memories of
fleeting beings?

I'm projecting.
A tree falls but no one is around to hear it.
Now it's a table. Now it's my heart
& everything my fingertips brush.

I'm not sure which feels worse—
leaving something aware of its loneliness,
or leaving nothing at all.

I'm talking about desire

Along a dirt road in spring
I feel the thumping
of male grouse.

It's a mating call and I wonder
how that works on
lady grouses.

I think I'm talking about desire.
I mean desire
to mate.

Lady grouses haven't much
to gain from the whole
lousy affair

but a satisfaction of instinct
to increase the grouse
population.

A motivation so deeply rooted
it never fully forms
to grown idea

in the lady grouse mind.
No introspection,
all action.

I'm talking about desire.
I think it must
be nice.

Becca Downs

My Mom Has No Grandkids So Every Conversation Ends with Death

The noon sun and drip of snowmelt from roof to road easements, little streams of almost-Spring, pulls me from that February Funk-type hibernation of the heart and body, known well by anyone who grew up where winters are endlessly gray. I walk to the neighborhood park, populated by gangs of geese and folks soaking in the sun on their lunch break. Call my mom as I do when I'm seeking an audience or to be one. We start with the weather, which doesn't count as small talk when we do it. More like scene-setting, establishing backdrops to make up for the hundreds of miles between us. I steer into the gory details of my recent food poisoning, and she reciprocates with a distant memory of her last major digestive disturbance. Something about the way she describes the "fancy house" where my dad hammed it up for other guests, how she grabbed his arm and with uncharacteristic aggression said We have to leave now, felt young, like a version of them I see only shadows of today. I ask how old she was. "Let's see. I'd say you and your brother were around six and four." The loop around the neighborhood lake takes me past a man pushing a stroller, a baby wrapped snug. Bare tree limbs scratching blue sky. Another man speaking in a hushed voice on the phone. Brown cattails stiff at the lake's edge. My mom tells me about the house my brother put an offer on. "I know how you feel about that, but it is cute. I'll send you the listing so you can see." I mhmmed. She knows how I feel about the future, and admits it's hard sometimes to see the point in recycling or refusing plastic straws. "It's not like I have grandkids anyway." Meaning the worth of years ahead is measured in generations. Meaning the people who have the most reason to care often don't, and she sometimes resents that. Meaning it's ok your divorce ended childless, good even. Meaning I'm sorry you ever felt pressure to be married. Meaning here is solace and olive branch. A few blocks later, nearly home now (home for now), I agree, "It's hard for younger generations to feel optimistic about the future." It's why we live in the now, I add, which happens to coincide with the future our parents planned for. "Look at us!" she cheers the mood, trying to match the sunshine pouring around me. "Your brother buying a house, you traveling around, and your dad and I looking into buying a camper. We're living our best lives right now!" Meaning this is the silver lining. Meaning we are on a precipice, we don't know what comes next. Meaning we're going to pretend this is the future a twenty-something mother of two, racing home to vomit as quietly as possible while her husband pays the babysitter, imagined: her son settling thousands of miles away, her daughter unsettled anywhere reciting how unlivable parts of the world will be in 20 years, and she and her husband making more effort to see them both. Meaning this is the future I married and gave birth to, and I will love it unconditionally. Meaning please love this future with me, I need you to love it with me. Love it now. Hundreds of thousands of dollars and hours invested in today. Look at us. Living our best lives. My hand clutches cold keys in my jacket pocket. God, would I ever love anyone enough to measure my years in theirs?

Why Does Everyone Still Think I'm Not Angry

When someone challenges
Me to write angrier
I wonder if they've been listening
To the breeze, the river, the trees
How they take everything in-
Side themselves and bear
The curse of remembering
Every flick of flint, each
Rush of electric-burdened gust.

Like a montane forest
I am full of fury
When I scream the western
Wind whips my breath into light
Clouds that drift slow
Over rivers, echo their
Riversongs. My scream-
Clouds hang still
Over tepid pine trees
Every afternoon. It's a magic
Trick I can't undo.

But I know the breeze lifts mad
Billows from the river which
Washes the tired feet of trees
Which stroke and ease
The weary wind. All things full
Of fury can also balm.

Wolf Licking Wound

I feel you tussle with ghosts
who look like bed sheets
taste like metal, sound like low
moan and wolf licking wounds.

They are ghosts of you, all
past lives lingering like one-
night lovers too long in bed
you don't know how to invite

to leave, maybe don't want to.
Ghosts, after all, are near
real, waft scent of whispers
so sweet and solemn you

forget they can't lull you
away from here, don't vanish
when you cry. That's the problem,
they multiply. You form a pack

of ghosts that suffocate you,
dog pile of every memory
you're supposed to release but
instead make casing of. Wrap

dangerous words inside the skin
of them. Consume. Satiate
a sadistic heart. I watch years
of ghosts sleep in your bed

while I   beside you.
I don't know which of us is
ghost anymore, so I beg
you to show them the door

before leaving each other
feels like wolf licking wound,
like daybreak in someone else's
bed and slipping out unnoticed.

Holding Funerals

Years-worth of road unspooled
between old hearts and mine
we could knit all the world

sweaters and together ask stars
whether our embraces–brief
now as we recall–happened at all

Were we only visions we dreamed,
dreams we slow danced with quiet
in dark living rooms, stories

scribbled in notebooks next morning,
mourned at the breakfast pyre
we observed on separate burners

confessions spilled from our lips
sizzled on the stove, gone the way
memories vanish when we stop

holding funerals for them.
Today the road before us still
spun tight in clenched fists–

would we dare relax and release,
roll like bones our fates
cross our fingers for each other's

roads to unravel forward
farther and farther
              apart

Becca Downs

waking next to her

campfire at daybreak

what a waste

(of their colors)

    some say

as if the flames

or the rising sun

should care

HOPE | ASH

is it such a   silly   thing
yes   wait is it
really so strange to look-
yes   wait is it
a fool's errand to look
    at ashes of a forest
& wonder if somewhere
    a garden   yes   wait
    if ashes could flower
is it childish to imagine

so many garden gnomes
such a   waste-
land everywhere parched
sucked dry and still
like pennies in a dry well
waiting to harness wind
spreading dead ash abroad
see new green light rising
unnaturally   we adjust
home in a   new world

Becca Downs

Generations of

this pain hovering, a
cloud of cologne coat,
warm but ghost-like
imprinted on me –

Grief is my mother now
no matter how I grow
she rocks me back
and forth, a queen

bed isn't big enough
for three, so it's only she
who comforts me
when sleep winks from her

far off constellation and
I am alone, a wake
for my dreams held by
everything I can't reach—

rocks smoothed by age
old waves, a moonlit
winter stroll, smoke creeping
shy out chimneys then

slinking to wherever only
coyotes can catch scent.
I have made a show
of Grief at my feet—

sunlight, garden, ash—
and Grief I can't see
for the thick fog I've given
breath and heartbeat—

union, certainty, child—
I have imprinted
on this performance,
placed a bow on her head,

gave her a name, watched
clouds sweep her up
in a show of their own
design. I called out for her

like stars or mountains
we speak to as daughters.
I wear a coat made of
cradle, crutch, prayer,

warm but ghost-like
for the way it reeks of
performance and blinds
like spotlight. I wear

everything for solace
we can birth the same
life and name we give
love as we give pain.

Skeleton and Cemetery

I hid my most dead plant behind books
so I wouldn't have to see her
dusty leaves curled and hunting
for water everywhere it wasn't.

Now she is skeleton and cemetery.
I see her sometimes when morning
air turns from dew and wet whisper
to sunbaked cement and I stand

to shut the window. I know I should end
her misery, return her to the earth. But
I'm afraid of tossing her crisp and decay
to the compost. I know what happens

next. I stand in sunlight with the kind
of pot with one purpose. Empty,
useless without new dirt and wiry roots.
A plot for new rot.

What fills an empty heart but that
which once drained it?
How long can I pretend a dead plant
isn't done dying yet?

I resent my fatigue, loathe the moments
of cactus stillness when I can't move
even the hairs on my neck. It seems
I can't even pour water for myself anymore.

I plant mystery seeds in new soil,
water from breath I still share, wait
child-like for magic sprouts to green
this worn world. What else could happen?

Finding Home

Home is where the heart-
you know what they say, and
a life worthwhile and well-lived-
there is a blueprint for this:

knowing the first step is to fall
in love, drowning-like you marry
ready for the hope of children
just enough invested in growing stocks,
bonds, a child's education, their blue-
print life-like fake money

that waits and waits and waits and

it pounds and relaxes and grips on cold
quilts next to a lover
which is to say you and I feel
our eyes lick each other clean, fine

like China or gold or the sun
the rest of the world all
left behind and spared
enough green grass, potable water, bail-
singed future we can't see, but
clutch like a desperate lover

dreams of holding another to keep living

Pulse

What is body
brain and breath
all for if not
to taste trees
river breeze
and each
other in hope-
ful moments
we're close
enough to feel
another heart
pulse

A Call to Arms

The sun opens arms to grass tucked between houses
this early August morning and I long to do the same.

To grow something
that could be bigger than me

I planted a sunflower in the brightest
spot in the front yard.

On this dewy morning she has reached
my height. Her petaled mane hangs low,

but I've seen her enliven at the sun's caress
and know she will soon surpass me.

So many like her perk at light
touch and I slump at the thought.

I have made a habit of jealousy, martyred
in direct sunlight for adoration, turned

and cursed the sun for burning my skin,
though I know he never claimed to only love

me with diaphragm or any quivering limb,
never held my hand to stop my finger-pointing.

I can't keep blaming his light for scorching me,
loosening himself instead upon a field of flowers

looking up. And to only grow
one big sunflower, give her all

the water, neglects life dwelling at her rooted feet—
wilting kale, crisping marigold.

I have resented the trellising vine loitering
worship-like around the water spout, reaching

skyward toward the sun, time-tested as sundial
and death. I have been cruel.

Starved the soil while jabbing a finger at the sun
too long. This yard thirsts

with patches where grasses should be
and the sun shouldn't be blamed for searing

the places I pretended I couldn't see.
I want to grow

more than one big thing. To nurture a land
that never belonged to me, brimming with flowers

unbound like bridal bouquet tossed
and caught in breeze, loosened

upon a once parched and vacant field. A call to arms
reaching skyward for a touch of resplendent love.

There Were No Children

When he left me for another woman and declared (divorce)
everyone said
Thank God there were no children.
Imagine how hard this would be if there were children.
and (I had to agree), robotically
I agreed each time.

Yes, thank God there were no children.
Yes, this would be so much harder if there were children.

(Daily still) I think about the babies we never had
we never conceived
because we weren't trying. But even when we weren't trying,
we were still trying.

The first time I mentioned a (late period) he greeted me
after work the next day with a pregnancy test from CVS
and waited outside the bathroom door while I (pissed)
on a stick.

Inside, just me and a stick and a moment (to confirm what I already knew).
Yes, this would be so much harder if there were (a child)

a moment

relief mixed with regret etched in the irises of his eyes.
Imagine how difficult this would be if there were children.
In the time between my (late period) and that moment
he had imagined a life with a child, (with our child),
the way I had imagined it from the moment I met him.
Yes, this would be so much harder if there were (children).
She toddles away with his toothbrush. She kicks
her first soccer ball with her tiny cleats. She sings tunes
in a language only she understands and we cannot keep our eyes off her.
Thank God there were no children.
He has his dad's jaw line. My freckles. He laughs
the same surprising, uncontrolled way we both did
when our lives were green like late spring.
Thank God there were no children.

We danced this routine again and again,
as if surprised our (birth) control methods were working,
the same way our friends were surprised when, like a ticking clock,
they each disrobed (birth control) and became pregnant.
                    This would be so much (harder if there were children).

It happens seemingly at random—I'm driving
the two-hour stretch between my parents'
new one-story home, Thank God, and my new-to-me
one-bedroom apartment, the highway whirring
there were beneath tires, cornfields stretching
to the horizon under distant gray storm clouds, no,
stark against the unhindered sunlight directly above
children. My parents have an extra guest room,
just in case, but they never ask about (children

anymore). Anyway,
it happens like a summer rain—sudden, wild, gone.
I weep, speak the refrain to no one:

Thank God there were no children.
Thank God there were no children.
Thank God there were no children.
Thank God there were no children.
Thank God there were no children.
Thank God there were no children.
Thank God there were no children.
Thank God there were no children.
Thank God there were no children.

Airborne Acid Rain

I am trying to die
alongside the rest of you

with grace—warm my face
sunward, slither my arms
wind-like around a twilight

lover, kiss waves as they smack
my face, I am trying to do this

while imagining a life without
my parents, my brother, anyone
who loves me

back. The thought of that
loss is a November gale,

will sink a ship and drown a crew,
boom like aftershock, last
like forest fire, outlast

most insects, will hover the planet,
make villains of us all, kill

us slowly like airborne
acid rain. We are all reaching
for an end. I am next to you reaching

for the violet-blue hue cresting
the end. I am reaching

for mountain melt dripping crystal
I am trying to fall in love
in case love and all else

I've ever known dies before
I do.

Becca Downs

Epithalamium for a New Age

I wanted to wrap this
gently, mercy at the foot
note, but I hired someone
mother-like to remind
who said you have to

forgive? It's true
we keep over-
paying our dues. He,
coughing up illness
in currency I trade

carefree on the wind,
me in hours stretching
silent nights out of sync
with sleep, sick or
shacking up with

the world. We can't see
for all the white light,
speak for the salt
papering our throats,
so let our lives river

sea-ward, like albatross
like November gale
like budding lovers
embracing for eternity
this emerald hue

this acid rain cascading
fractured streets,
reinventing color
of flowers, and us
heiresses releasing the end

of the world
we once knew, reaching
to the new breeze rising
pink with the morning sun.

ACKNOWLEDGEMENTS

I'd like to thank the following literary magazines and publishers for kindly housing some of the poems in this manuscript.

Glass Mountain - "Her into Himself"

Jupiter Review - "Borders"

Eclectica - "The Shape of Things"

Flying Island Literary Journal - "Peace Offerings"

Heartland Society of Women Writers - "Caged-Tiger the Tide Pools," "Awakening, Again," and "No Name Here"

South Broadway Ghost Society - "Acid Rain Epithalamium"

Twenty Bellows - "Acid Rain Epithalamium," "Modern Climate/Love Disasters," and "HOPE | ASH," as well as "Burning Age" (nominated for a 2024 Pushcart Prize) and "Lullaby" in the anthology We Are the West

Beyond the Veil Press - "Woman as Cloud Performer"

I'd also like to thank my mentors and workshop leaders–Carolina Ebeid, Khadijah Queen, and Suzi Q. Smith–as well as my incredible poetry cohort in the Regis University Mile-High MFA program for their guidance, wisdom, and support. David, Megan, Ashley, Laura, Jessie, Michelle, Confidence–you all have touched these poems and I'm forever grateful for that. Thank you also to Andrea Rexilius, Eric Baus, Rachel Weaver, and everyone else on faculty at the Mile-High MFA program.

My incredibly talented and supportive undergrad professors helped me reach this point, too. Thank you Terry Kirts for your constant support and guidance throughout my undergraduate years, during my divorce (I'm eternally grateful you let me sit in on your graduate creative nonfiction course while I was enduring divorce–it helped me dream myself back to life), and as I applied to MFA programs. David Beck–thank you for inviting me into your book club and always being a professional and academic reference. Mitchell Douglas–you likely don't remember the quiet girl in your Intro to Poetry course back in 2011, but she will never forget the way poetry suddenly became accessible, beautiful, and powerful under your guidance.

Thank you to Sage Herrin, Tyler Hurula, and Beyond the Veil Press for believing in this book and putting in so much work to bring it into the world. You have been a dream to work with.

And of course, this manuscript wouldn't be here without the love and support of my friends and family–especially my parents, Phil and Joleen, and my brother, Gavin. The worst thing to happen to me became the best thing to happen to me, and these poems were borne in the wake of that journey. Thank you forever and ever for being part of that journey.

About The Author

Becca Downs (she/they) is a writer, editor, educator, poet, and graduate of the Mile-High MFA program at Regis University. They lead creative writing workshops throughout Denver, where they live with their chosen Queen City Cooperative family. Born in Fort Wayne, Indiana, Becca is grateful for her Hoosier roots, family, and friends, and is passionate about strengthening community wherever she lives.

Follow their journey on Instagram: @beccad____
Website: beccadownswriting.com

About The Press

Beyond The Veil Press is a queer trans disabled-led indie publisher of poetry & art focused on mental health awareness. Based on the lands of the Kumeyaay.(San Diego, CA)

Since we began in 2021 (Cheyenne/Ute/Arapaholands – Denver, CO) the press has grown to offer community resources through writing workshops, writing retreats, open mics, and community events.

Visit beyondtheveilpress.com to sign up for the Mewsletter, and follow our Instagram @beyondtheveilpress for submission calls, events, virtual mics, workshops, & more!

Other Titles From Beyond The Veil Press

Acid Rain Epithalamium by Becca Downs
Anti/Muse: Poems by Sage Herrin & Art by Josiah Callaway
As Long As This Heart Beats by Kyrsta Morehouse
Dear Survivor Zine Series: living with PTSD by Sage Herrin
Delicate Things by Shannon English & Art by Gabriela Ponce Curlango
Heretic: A Story of Spiritual Liberation in Poems by Kristy Webster
I Can Make Love Poems Out of Anyone (Zine) by Sage Herrin
Listening Party: House Music and Other Conversations by Robbie Robinson
Maybe She's Born With It, Maybe It's Trauma by Cait Thomson
Surviving Peter Pan by Marissa Forbes
Taking Back the Body by Talicha J.
The Shattered Muse by Sage Herrin & Art by Josiah Callaway
Through The Red Door's Open Maw by Jess Cato
TRANSabdominal Retrieval by Teddy Goetz
We Are Creatures Of What Has Happened by Ashley Mezzano
Yoni Provenance by Susan Niemi & Art by Joan Green

Anthology 01: There Is A Monster Inside That I Am Learning To Love
Anthology 02: Tea With My Monster
Anthology 03: How To Heal A Bloodline
Anthology 04: We Apologize for the Inconvenience – LGBTQ+
Anthology 05: Do Not Tap On The Glass
Anthology 06: Relics of Unbearable Softness – LGBTQ+
Anthology 07: Songs from Another Sun – BIPOC
Anthology 08: Dear Survivor: Reclaim the light – Survivors of Sexual Assault
Anthology 09: We Do Not Need Permission To Rise - LGBTQ+
Anthology 10: In Praise of Despair – Disability Pride Anthology
Anthology 11: America Does Not Exist – LGBTQ+

Mental Health Resources We Love

BOOKS

Permission to come home: reclaiming mental health as Asian Americans - Jenny Wang

The Pain We Carry: Healing from C-PTSD for People of Color - Natalie Gutierrez

Journey Through Trauma: Healing Repeated Trauma - Gretchen Schmelzer

The Deepest Well - Dr. Nadine Burke Harris

My Grandmother's Hands - Resmaa Menakem *tw: police violence

What My Bones Know - Stephanie Foo (memoir)

The Journey From Abandonment To Healing – Susan Anderson

Waking The Tiger - Peter Levine

Polysecure: Attachment, Trauma, & Consensual Nonmonogamy – Jessica Fern

Self-Therapy: Guide to Healing Your Inner Child Using IFS - Jay Early

The Body Keeps The Score – Bessel van der Kolk

WEBSITES

AFSP.org - Saving lives and bringing hope to those affected by suicide.

TheTrevorProject.org - for LGBTQ+ youth.

RAINN.org - for survivors of sexual assault

Equip.health - online eating disorder treatment and resources

PODCASTS

Where Is My Mind? – Niall Breslin

The Hilarious World of Depression; Depreche Mode – John Moe

The Happiness Lab – Dr. Laurie Santos

Speaking of Psychology – Kim I. Mills

Being Well – Dr. Rick Hanson and Forrest Hanson

SAMHSA National Helpline
1-800-662-HELP (4357)

National Alliance on Mental Illness (NAMI) HelpLine
1-800-950-NAMI (6264)

Crisis Text Line
Text 741741

National Domestic Violence Hotline
1-800-799-SAFE (7233) or text "LOVEIS" to 22522

National Eating Disorders Association (NEDA) Helpline
1-800-931-2237
Rape Abuse and Incest National Network (RAINN)
1-800-656-HOPE (4673)

LGBT National Hotline
1-888-843-4564

The Trevor Project
1-866-488-7386 or Text "START" to 678678

Thank you for reading!
Be gay, do poetry